FUNK/JAZZ BASS

THE BEST SINGLE SOURCE FOR LEARNING TO PLAY LIKE THE MASTERS

by Jon Liebman

Bass tracks: Jon Liebman

Guitar tracks, drum programming, and audio production: Adam Liebman

To access video visit:
www.halleonard.com/mylibrary

Enter Code
6868-0904-0831-5925

T0084215

ISBN 978-1-5400-6045-7

Hal•Leonard®

Copyright © 2022 by HAL LEONARD LLC
International Copyright Secured   All Rights Reserved

No part of this publication may be reproduced in any form or by
any means without the prior written permission of the Publisher.

Visit Hal Leonard Online at
www.halleonard.com

Contact us:
Hal Leonard
7777 West Bluemound Road
Milwaukee, WI 53213
Email: info@halleonard.com

In Europe, contact:
Hal Leonard Europe Limited
42 Wigmore Street
Marylebone, London, W1U 2RN
Email: info@halleonardeurope.com

In Australia, contact:
Hal Leonard Australia Pty. Ltd.
4 Lentara Court
Cheltenham, Victoria, 3192 Australia
Email: info@halleonard.com.au

FOREWORD

BY NATHAN EAST

When I think of all the possibilities when creating a great bass line, it's fascinating to see what different players come up with, especially when they're all within the same genre.

In *Funk/Jazz Bass*, Jon Liebman has compiled a phenomenal cross section of players and composed his own interpretations, capturing the essence, uniqueness, and personality of each one. A task like that is no small feat, and Jon absolutely nails it!

My friend Jon Liebman gets right to the core of what's important for a bass player, through his books and online bass instruction series. He understands the value of laying down a solid groove and making the music "feel good."

This book is an asset to any bassist with a desire for an expanded vocabulary of grooves, ideas, fills, and more. I'm truly honored to have been included in this collection, alongside so many of my bass heroes.

Congratulations, Jon, on another exceptional resource for bass players. Well done, my friend!

Nathan East is a Grammy Award-winning bassist, vocalist, composer, and solo artist. Over the course of his brilliant career, Nathan has performed and/or recorded with everyone from Barry White, George Harrison, Michael Jackson, Whitney Houston, and Stevie Wonder to Barbra Streisand, B.B. King, Elton John, Aretha Franklin, Natalie Cole, George Benson, Quincy Jones, and countless others. He has also done extensive tours with Kenny Loggins, Al Jarreau, Herbie Hancock, Toto, Phil Collins, Eric Clapton, and his own contemporary supergroup Fourplay.

INTRODUCTION

The purpose of this book is to illustrate the numerous possibilities of playing funk/jazz bass by analyzing how the bass greats have done it.

With so much incredible bass talent out there, I thought it would be a good idea to home in on what some of these incredible bass players have been doing, what their styles have in common, and where they differ.

Most people would probably describe "funk/jazz," logically, as a melding of funk and jazz. Others might go so far as to call it jazzed-up funk, or funked-up jazz. Regardless of the words, it's fascinating to hear so many different sounds and feels created by bass players within the funk/jazz milieu, as you're about to find out.

Throughout these pages, I've presented a compilation of grooves in the styles of 30 of the most celebrated funk/jazz bass players in music history. Though all the pieces in this book can be classified as "funk/jazz," the variety of approaches from the players represented is nothing short of amazing.

Much thought went into selecting the individuals that are highlighted in this book. To include every influential funk/jazz bassist would require a book far too lengthy. Narrowing the list down to 30 people was a daunting task. Each bassist was chosen not only for his or her unique contributions to funk/jazz bass playing, but also to showcase the individual approaches they personify.

Some of the music selections lean more toward the funk side, while others are jazzier. There's a wide variety of stylistic expression and nuance too, including slapping, chord playing, "dead" note articulation, and fretless-oriented grooves. You'll find heavy doses of R&B, a bit of Latin, and even a little hip-hop influence sprinkled in as well.

This book is sure to expand your groove vocabulary and will help you make great strides in your bass technique. I've included online video demonstrations of all 30 selections too, as a guide to help you play each piece correctly. To access the videos, you'll find a URL with your personal code on page 1 of this book.

What a humbling experience it is to pay homage to this select group of funk/jazz bass greats. I hope you enjoy playing the music in this book as much as I enjoyed writing it.

– Jon Liebman

CRITICAL ACCLAIM

"My friend Jon Liebman gets right to the core of what's important for a bass player. A task like that is no small feat, and Jon absolutely nails it!"

– Nathan East (Eric Clapton, Whitney Houston, Fourplay)

"The bass lines Jon has written for this book will help any bass player analyze and understand the approaches used by a variety of bassists. I am so honored to be a part of this project!"

– Alain Caron (UZEB, Mike Stern, Billy Cobham)

"This book is a great tool for all bass players. I highly recommend it! Thank you, Jon, for doing a great job."

– Carlitos Del Puerto (Chick Corea, Gloria Estefan, Bruce Springsteen)

"A great book, with a lot of great exercises. All aspiring bass players should have it!"

– Bunny Brunel (Herbie Hancock, Wayne Shorter, Dizzy Gillespie)

"*Funk/Jazz Bass* exposes an excellent view of these music genres, as well as great respect for the bass players who are referenced. It is an informative book, definitely worth having!"

– Chuck Rainey (Aretha Franklin, Steely Dan, Quincy Jones)

"This book is amazing! I'm so excited to be part of it with all these great bass players. What a great educational book for the next generation. Thanks, Jon, and congratulations, my friend!"

– Bakithi Kumalo (Paul Simon, Randy Brecker, Bob James)

1. VICTOR BAILEY

Victor Bailey was highly revered for his stature as a grooving bass player, both as a sideman and a solo artist. Though he's no longer with us, Victor will forever be remembered as the person brave enough to replace the inimitable Jaco Pastorius in Weather Report, helping to lead the band in a new direction. Victor's style included innovative scale runs, intricate fills, and masterful slapping.

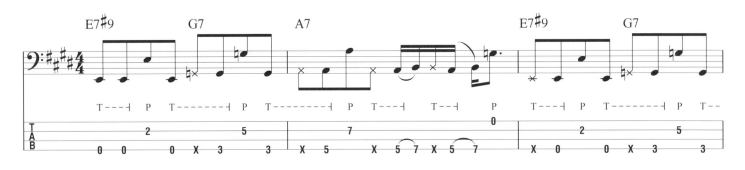

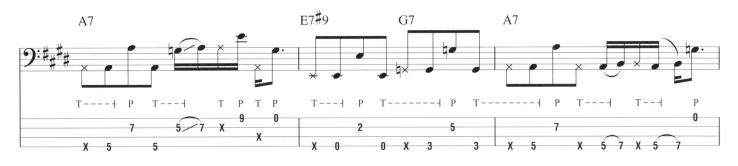

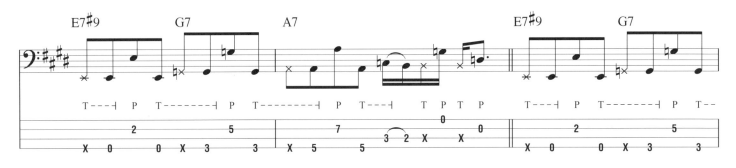

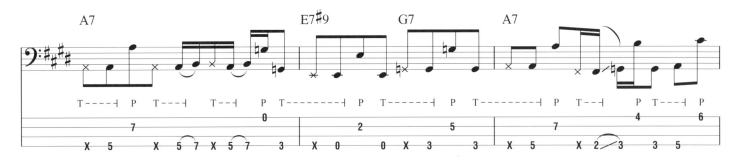

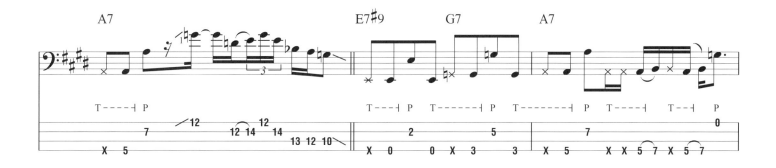

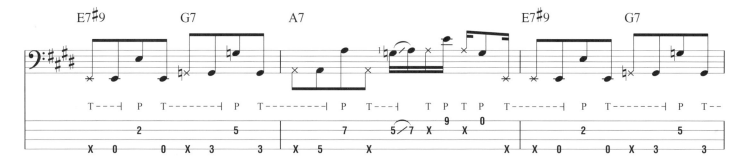

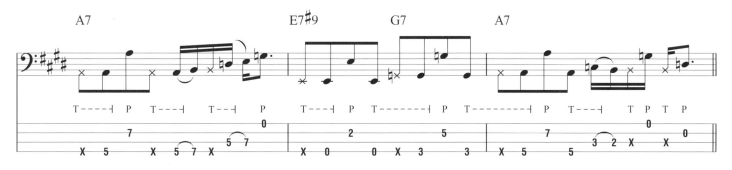

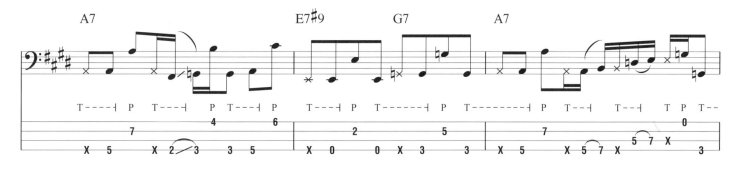

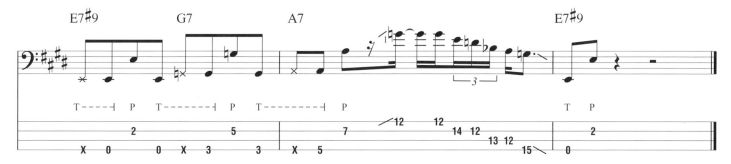

2. JEFF BERLIN

Heralded as one of the most extraordinary bassists of his generation, Jeff Berlin has performed extensively with Bill Bruford, Allan Holdsworth, and many others, in addition to releasing several acclaimed records as a leader. His stellar bass technique frequently makes use of sustained 16th-note passages and "dead" notes.

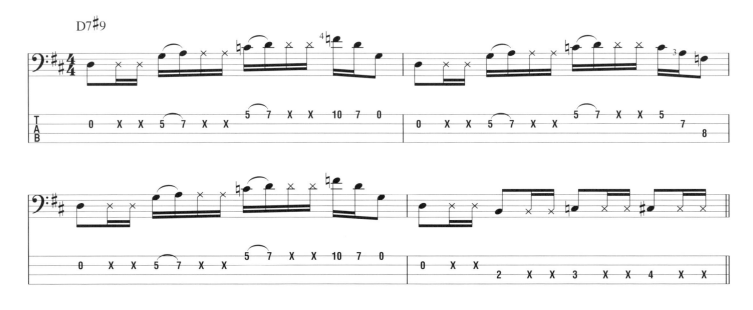

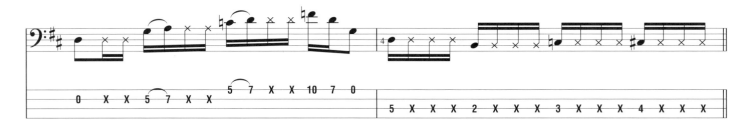

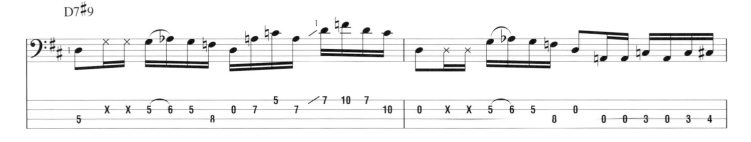

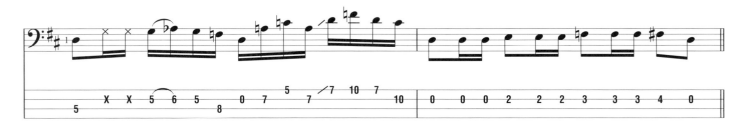

6

3. RICHARD BONA

A native of Cameroon, Richard Bona has wowed audiences all over the world with his unique and energetic approach to the bass guitar. Bona's playing highlights an affinity for taking simple chord progressions, often Latin-tinged, and inserting percussiveness, creative scale fills, ghost notes, and chords.

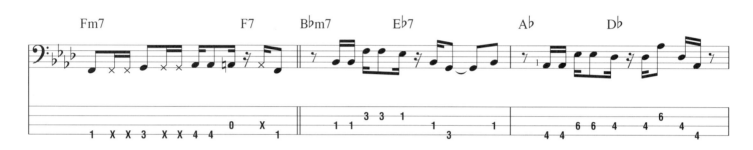

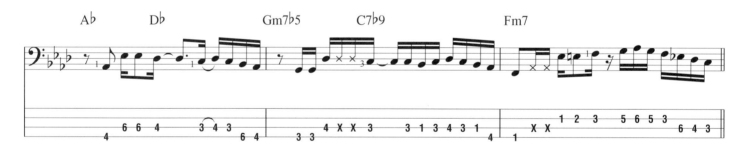

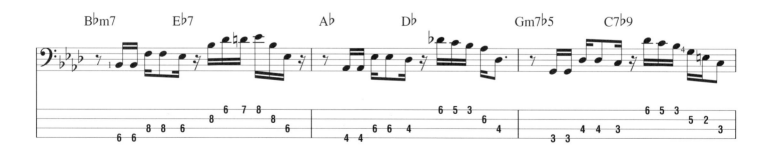

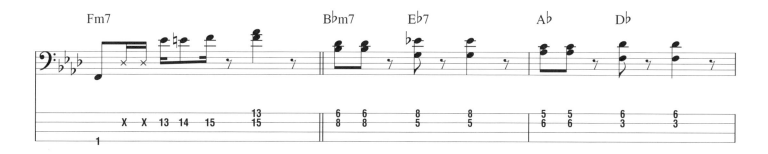

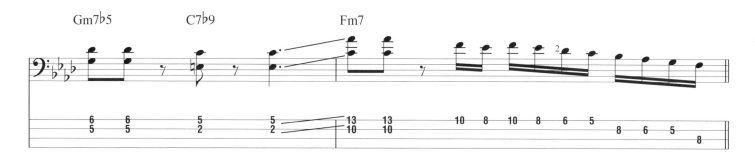

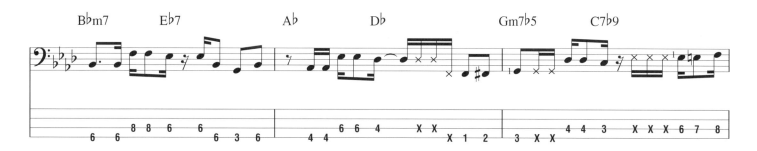

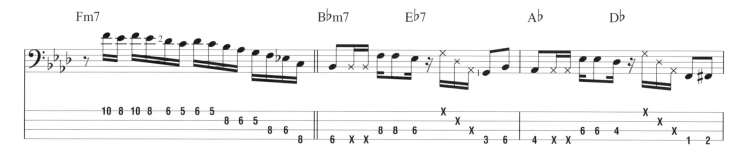

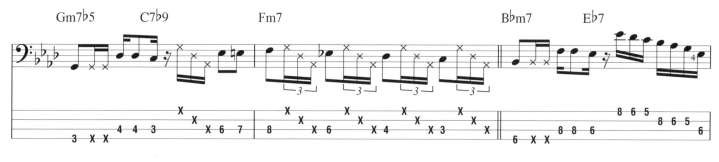

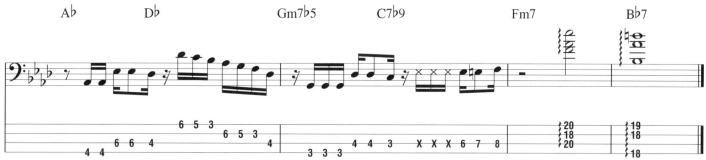

4. BRIAN BROMBERG

A master of both the upright and electric bass, Brian Bromberg does it all. While his sideman credits read like a who's who of music icons (Stan Getz, Horace Silver...), Brian is also a prolific solo artist, having released dozens of albums as a leader. His playing includes blues-like licks, dazzling slapping displays, and virtuosic fills.

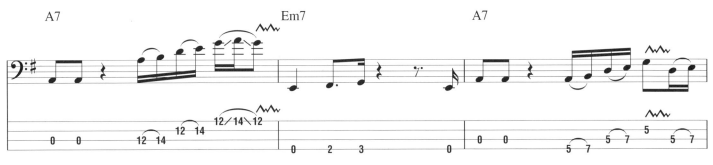

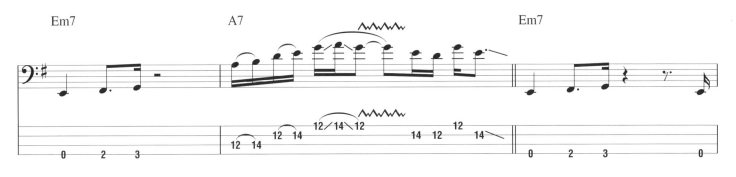

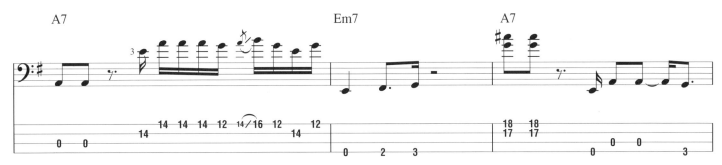

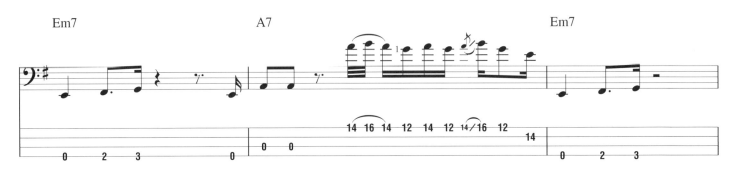

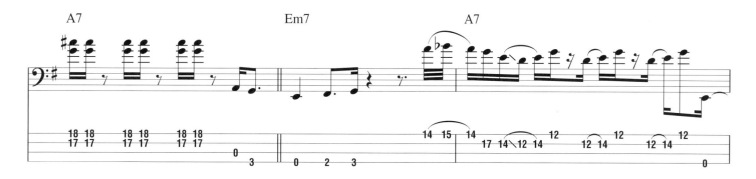

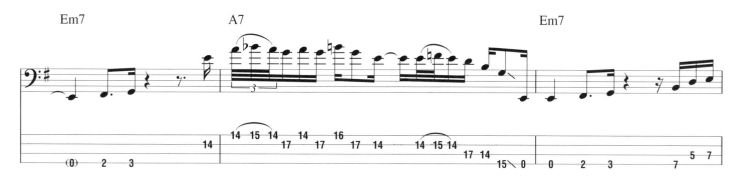

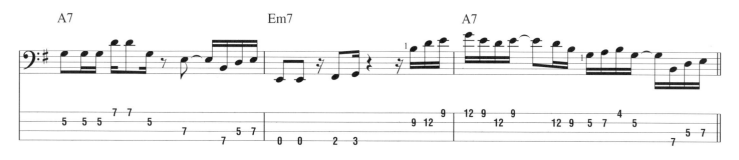

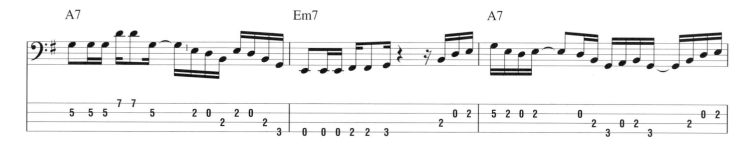

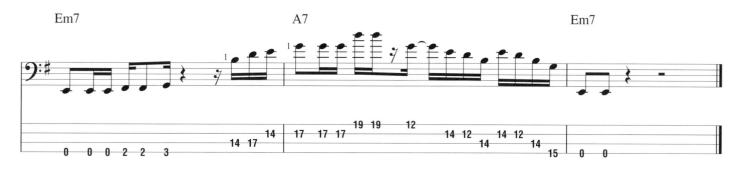

5. BUNNY BRUNEL

Hailing from France, Bunny Brunel is a world-renowned, multi-faceted bass player. Throughout his distinguished career, Bunny has recorded with Chick Corea, Natalie Cole, Dizzy Gillespie, and countless others. With fretless bass often his instrument of choice, Bunny makes full use of slides and vibrato, all the while injecting his own personality into his playing.

Best on Fretless

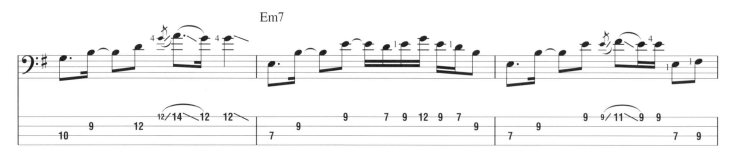

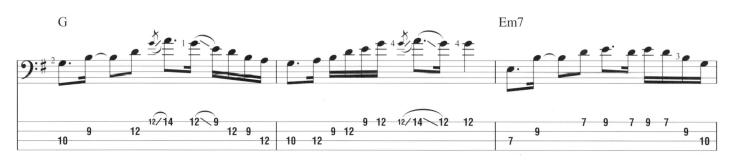

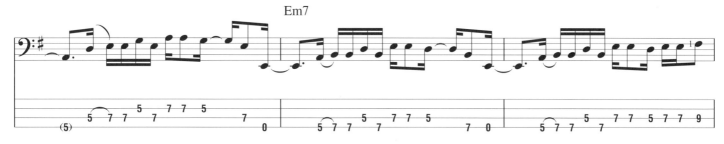

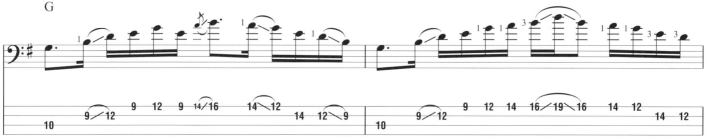

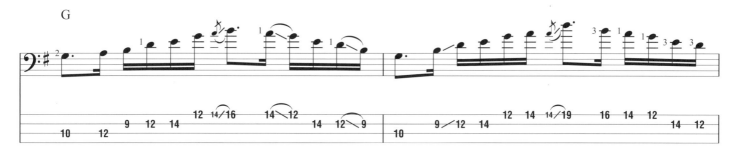

6. OTEIL BURBRIDGE

With a pedigree that includes Dead & Company, the Allman Brothers Band, and Tedeschi Trucks, Oteil Burbridge is a highly accomplished instrumentalist, demonstrating uncanny familiarity with virtually every aspect of the bass guitar. Whether he's laying down a nasty groove, playing a compelling solo, or injecting intricate fills, Oteil is as funky as they come.

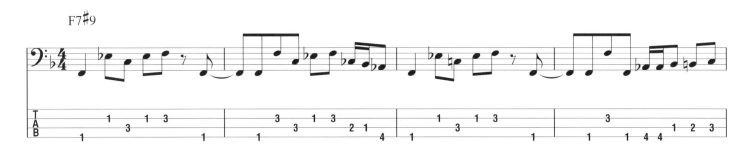

14

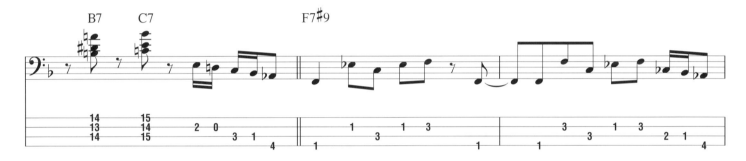

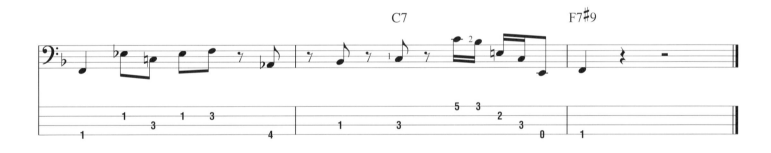

7. ALAIN CARON

Canadian bassist Alain Caron rose to international acclaim in the '80s as a member of the Montreal fusion band UZEB. He has also toured with the likes of Mike Stern, Billy Cobham, Biréli Lagrène, Dennis Chambers, and many others. Alain tends to favor a fretless bass, and his compositions frequently include unexpected changes in chord progressions. His funky, R&B-like grooves exemplify a marriage of jazz and funk.

Best on Fretless

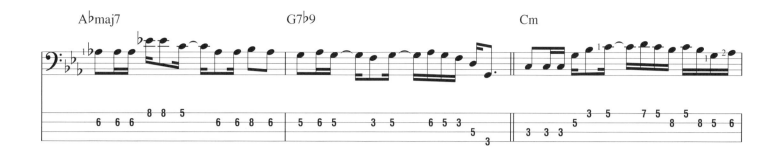

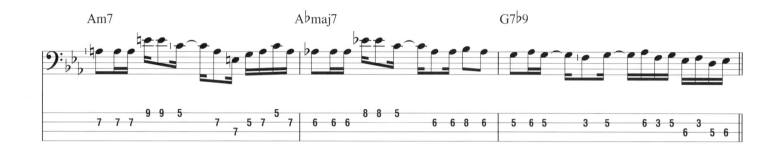

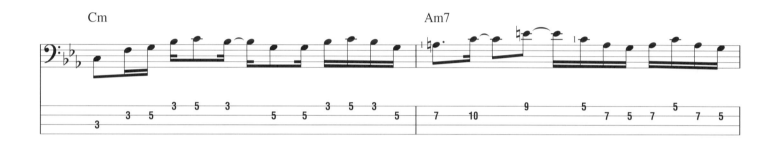

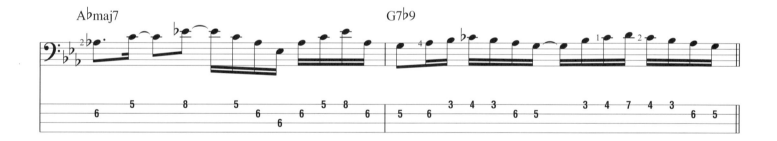

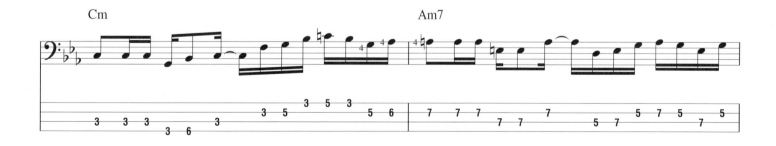

8. OSKAR CARTAYA

Having lived in Puerto Rico, New York, and Los Angeles, Oskar Cartaya has been immersed in Latin music culture virtually from the beginning. The acclaimed bassist/producer has worked with Arturo Sandoval, Willie Colón, Tito Puente, and many others. Oskar's playing personifies Latin bass funk at its finest.

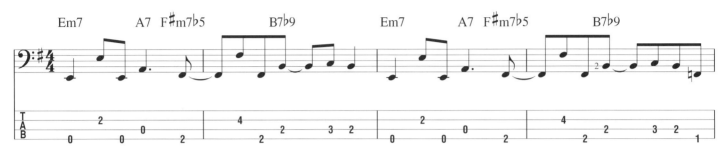

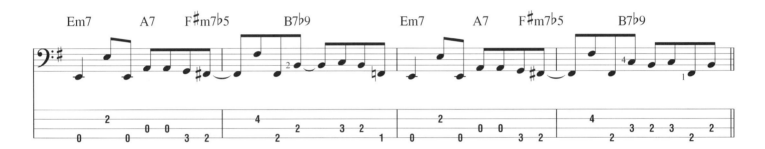

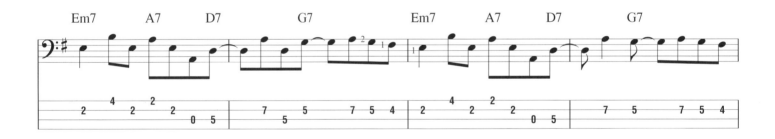

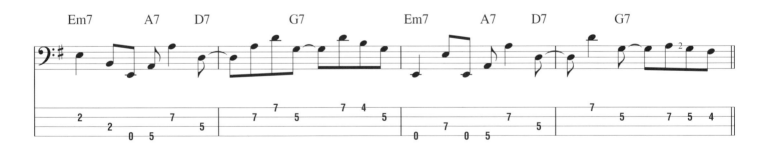

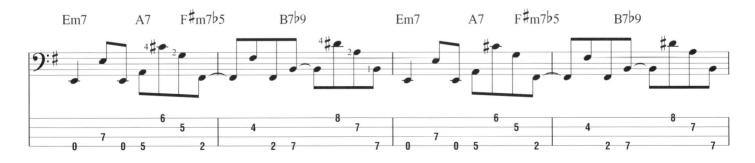

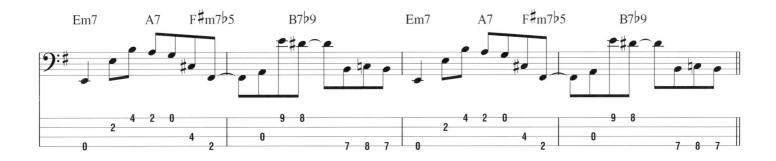

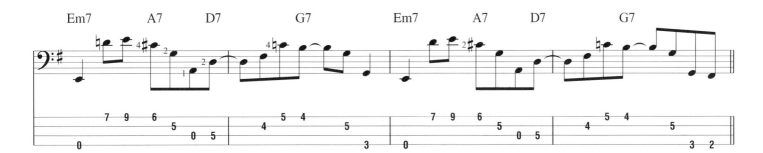

Repeat and fade

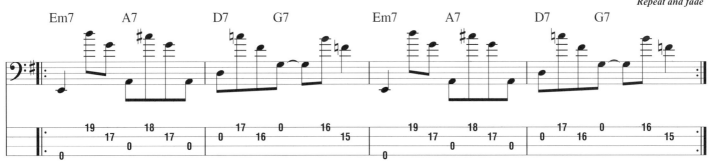

9. STANLEY CLARKE

A pioneer of the jazz/fusion scene in the 1970s, Stanley Clarke rose to prominence as a member of Chick Corea's Return to Forever band, which led to his standing as a leading jazz artist in his own right. Stanley's technical virtuosity incorporates blazing solos, double stops, and high-energy slapping, accentuated by frequent use of "dead" notes.

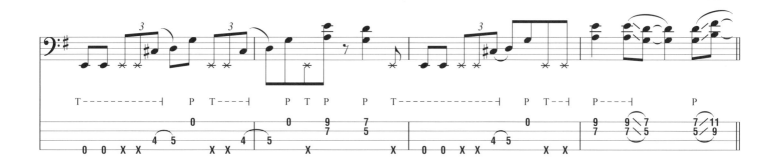

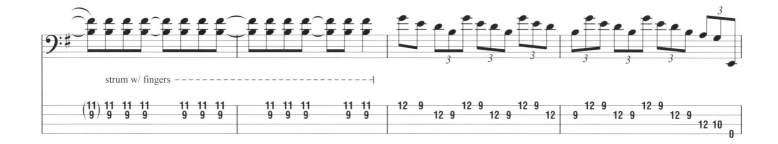

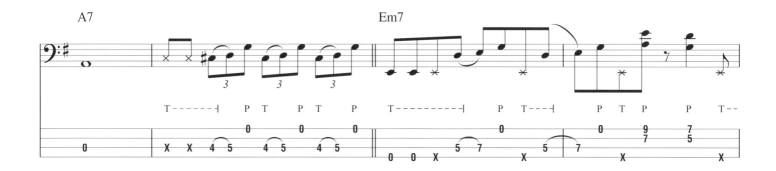

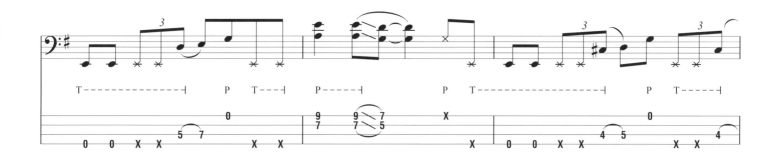

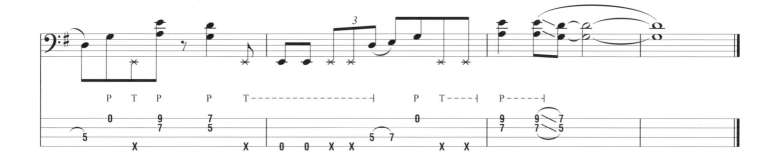

10. CARLITOS DEL PUERTO

One of the most in-demand bassists on the music scene today, Carlitos Del Puerto has worked with everyone from Chick Corea and Quincy Jones to Bruce Springsteen, Stevie Wonder, and Barbra Streisand. When it comes to Latin music, Carlitos comes by it honestly, as he is the son of Cuban bass legend Carlos Del Puerto. The syncopated rhythms and displaced beats in this piece typify Carlitos' approach to grooving.

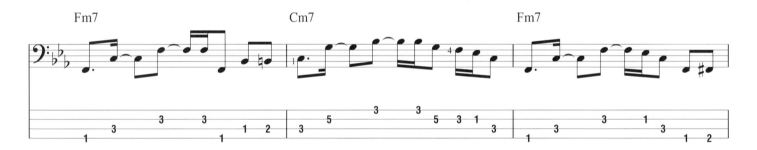

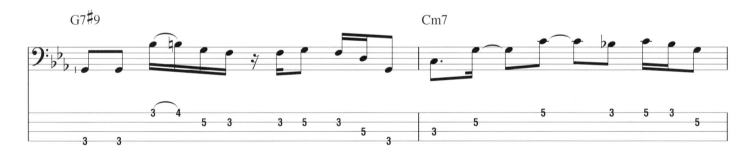

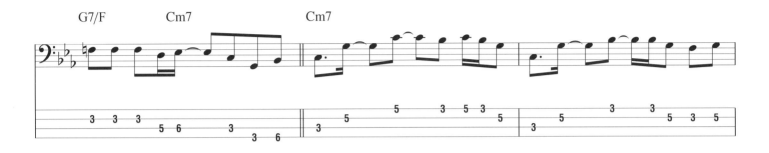

11. DAVID DYSON

Smooth groover David Dyson has performed with a long list of high-profile acts including George Duke, Lalah Hathaway, and Pieces of a Dream. His playing incorporates a variety of right-hand techniques including slapping, percussiveness, and double stops.

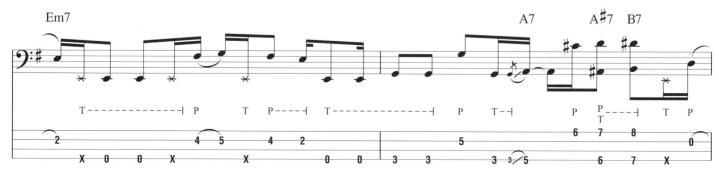

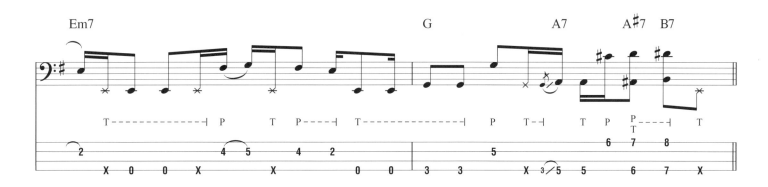

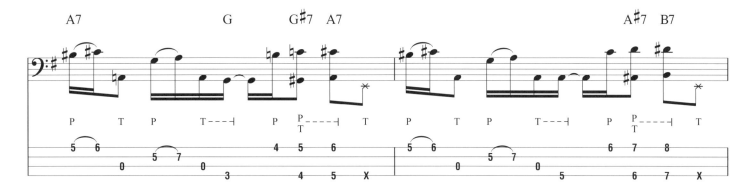

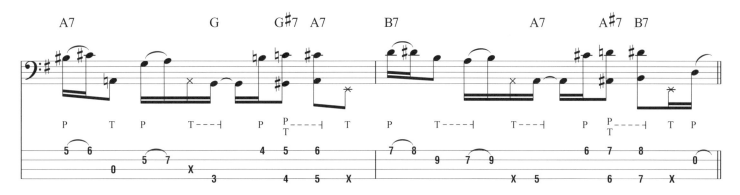

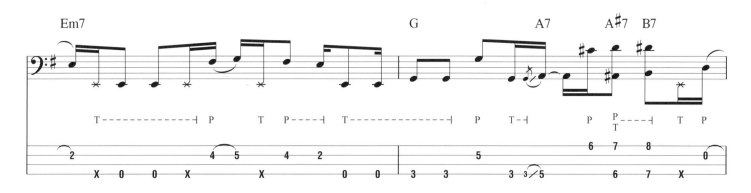

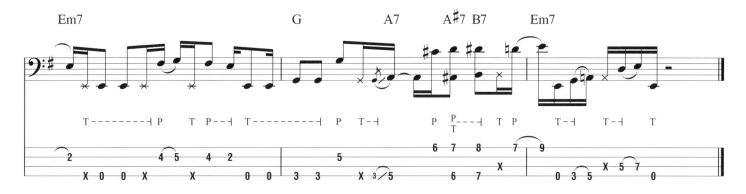

12. NATHAN EAST

With thousands of album credits and extensive work with Fourplay, Eric Clapton, Phil Collins, and countless others, Nathan East has been a major force in the jazz, R&B, and rock music scenes for decades. His ever-solid bass lines consistently provide just the "right" feel for whatever groove is at hand, often embellished with intricate scale runs, slides, and tasteful fills.

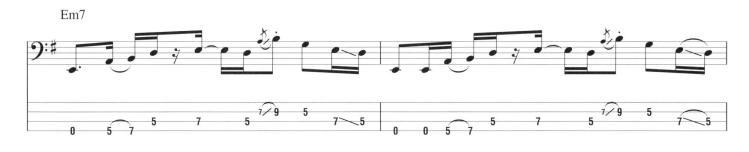

13. BERNARD EDWARDS

Bernard Edwards is remembered as one of the music world's most highly respected bass players. Co-founder, with Nile Rodgers, of the '70s funk and dance band Chic, Edwards incorporated syncopation, interval jumps, passing tones, and effective use of space into his bass lines, making him one of the funkiest groovers of all time.

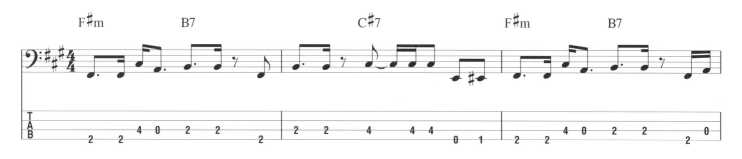

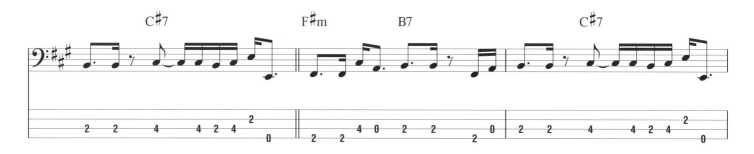

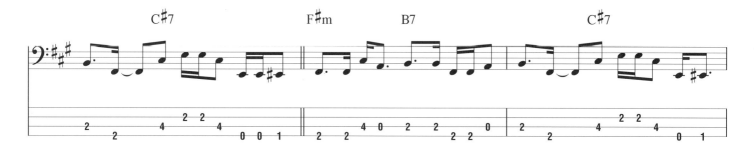

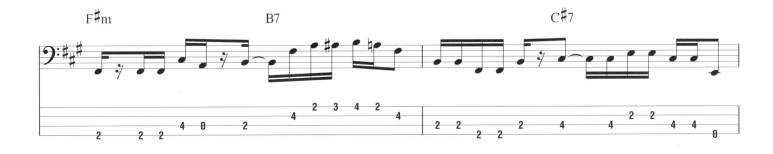

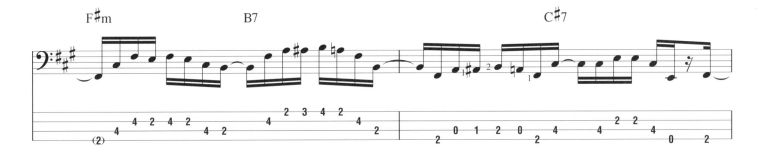

14. WILTON FELDER

A founding member of the jazz/fusion supergroup the Crusaders, Wilton Felder was widely known as both a saxophone player and an amazing bass groover. In addition to his prolific recording credits with the Crusaders, Felder's funky bass lines, with intricate 16th-note patterns, can be heard on iconic tracks with the Jackson 5, Marvin Gaye, Al Jarreau, and many others.

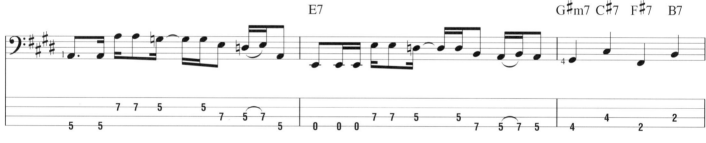

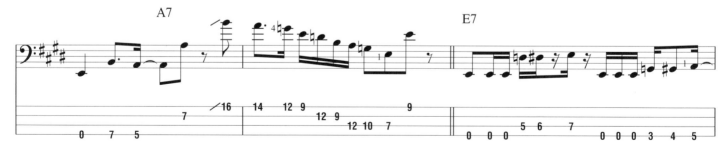

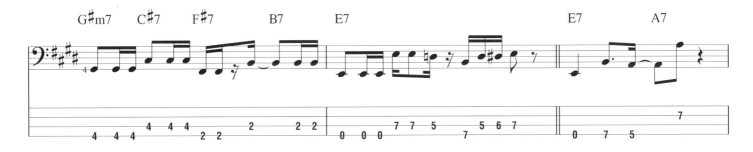

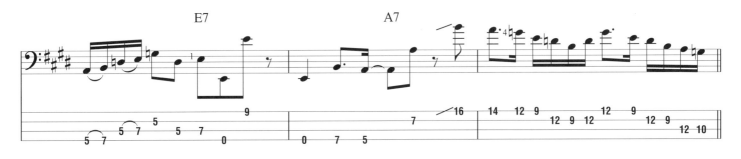

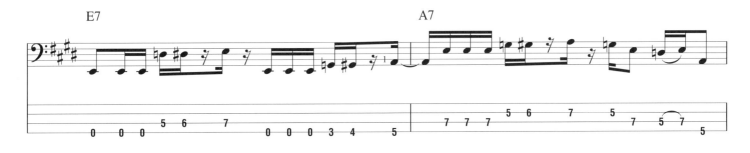

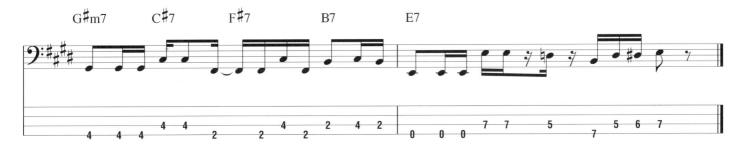

15. MATT GARRISON

Son of legendary jazz bassist Jimmy Garrison, Matt has taken the electric bass to a new level. The younger Garrison has recorded with Herbie Hancock, John McLaughlin, Dennis Chambers, and many others. His ever-creative bass lines feature nimble 16th-note runs, frequent use of "dead" notes, and double stops.

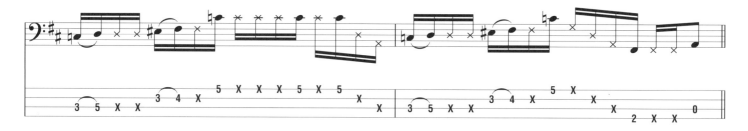

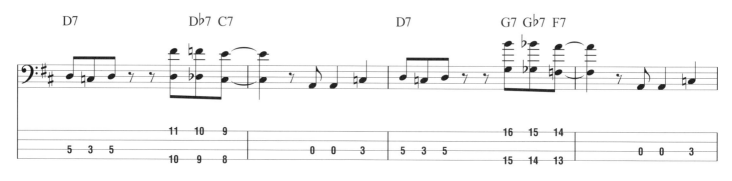

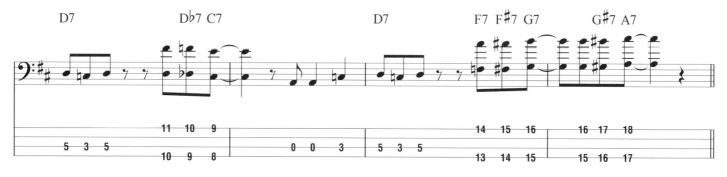

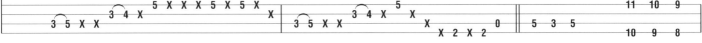

16. JIMMY HASLIP

A founding member of the jazz/fusion group the Yellowjackets, Jimmy Haslip has also worked as a bassist and/or producer with a long list of high-profile artists including Jeff Lorber, Allan Holdsworth, and Chaka Khan. Often preferring a fretless, the left-handed Haslip holds his basses like a lefty but maintains the "righty" stringing—essentially playing the bass upside down! Jimmy is constantly pushing the musical envelope, even finding ways to make pentatonic grooves more interesting, as demonstrated here.

Best on Fretless

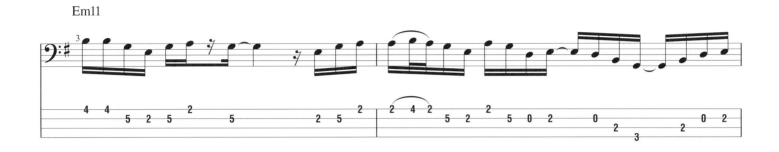

Em11

Em11

17. PAUL JACKSON

Paul Jackson is best known for his work with Herbie Hancock in the legendary Headhunters band. Jackson's grooves form a charging pulse of pure, natural funk, embellished with his strategic use of "dead" notes.

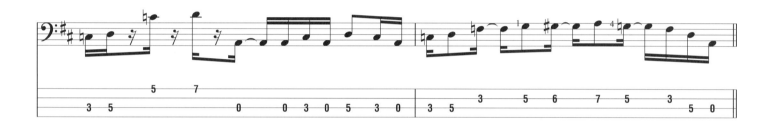

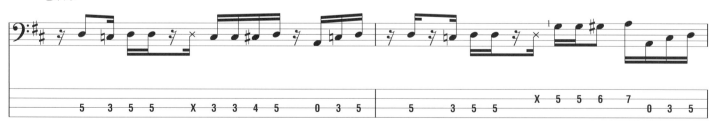

D7#9

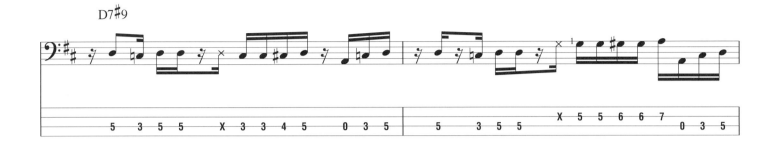

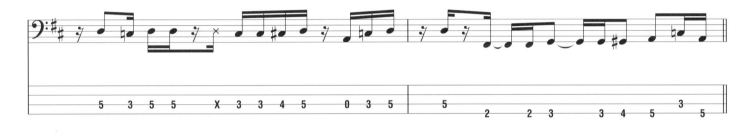

D7#9

18. JAMES JAMERSON

Considered by many to have been the greatest bass player ever, James Jamerson is best known for providing the driving beat behind many classic Motown hits. Jamerson's lines are often busy and full of interval jumps, follow a pulsating syncopation, and occasionally include non-chord tones.

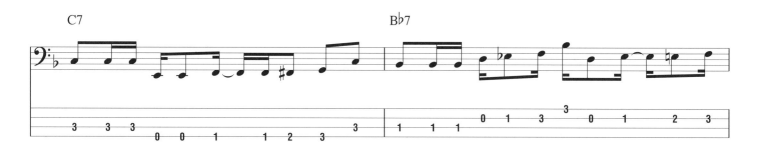

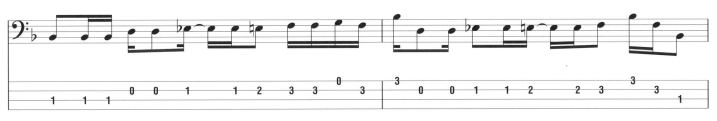

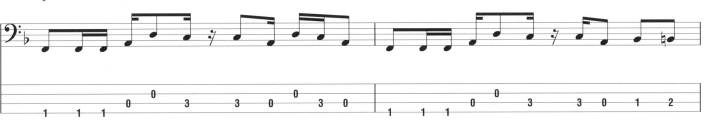

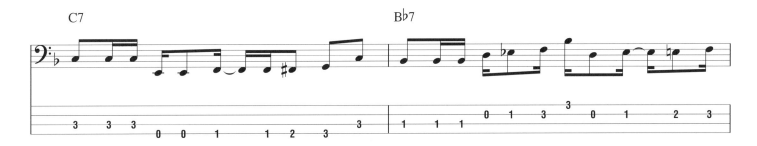

19. JERRY JEMMOTT

A highly influential bass player from the '60s and '70s, Jerry Jemmott has worked extensively with Aretha Franklin, B.B. King, Wilson Pickett, and many others. His funky, soul-filled bass lines make full use of scale runs, octave patterns, and syncopation.

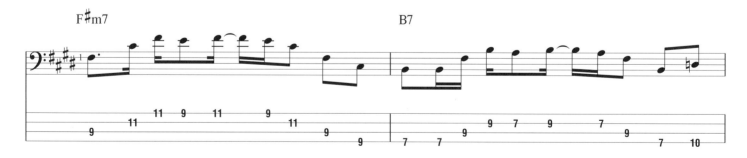

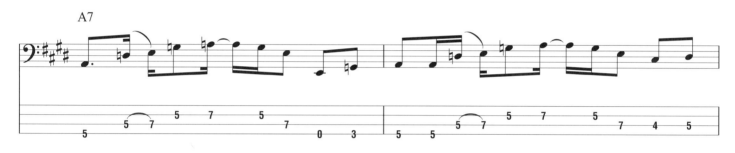

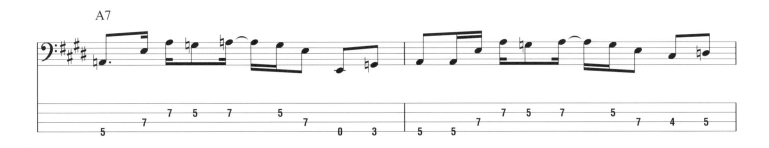

20. ALPHONSO JOHNSON

An early member of the seminal jazz/fusion band Weather Report, Alphonso Johnson also performed and recorded with Santana, Phil Collins, and Dee Dee Bridgewater, and as a solo artist. Often opting for a fretless bass, Alphonso's lines are funky and melodic. This piece, with a Latin feel, demonstrates how arpeggios can be incorporated into a grooving bass line.

Best on Fretless

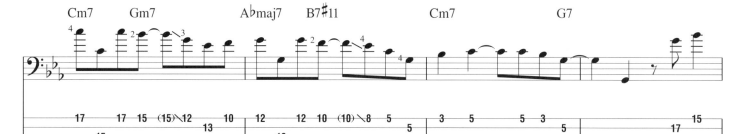

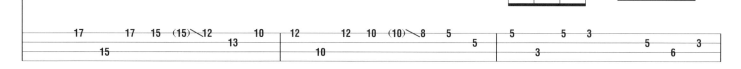

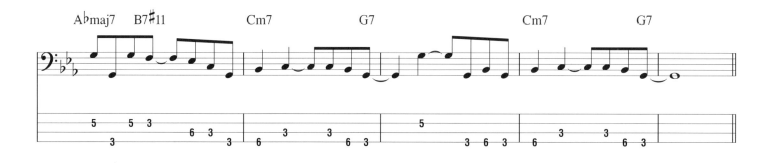

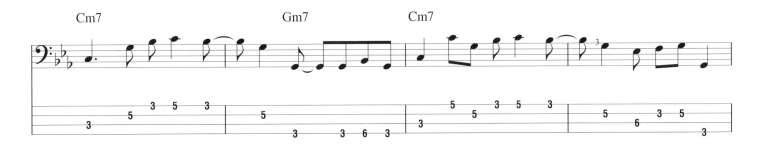

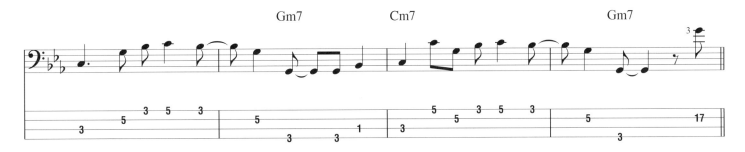

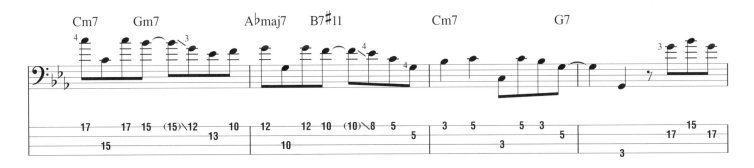

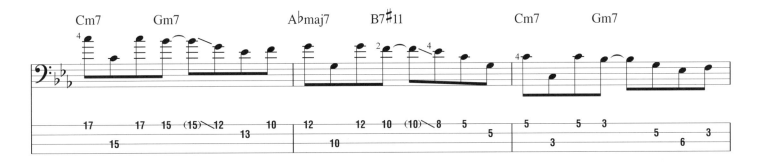

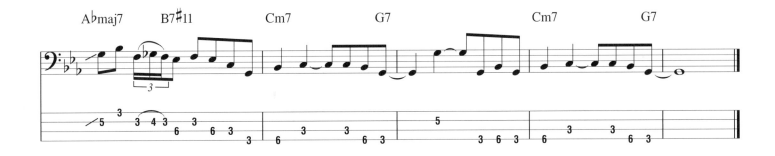

21. BAKITHI KUMALO

Born and raised in South Africa, Bakithi Kumalo was catapulted to worldwide acclaim when Paul Simon hired him to perform on his 1986 *Graceland* album. Largely known for his work on the fretless bass, Bakithi takes full advantage of the fretless fingerboard, incorporating slides and vibrato. He also perked up everyone's ears with his one-of-a-kind fretless slap technique!

Best on Fretless

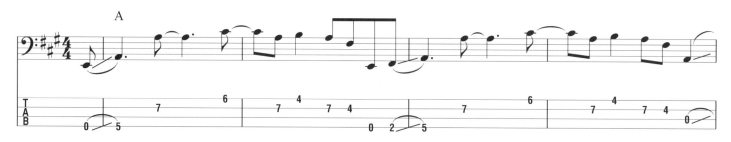

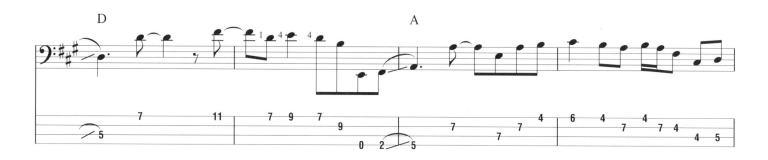

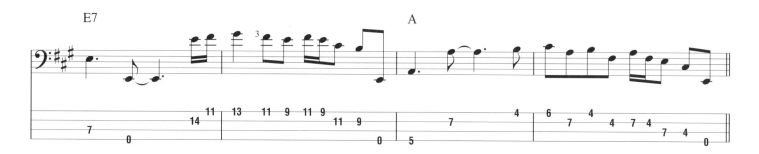

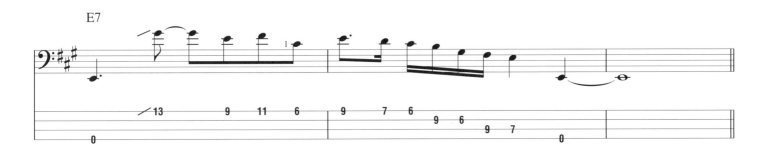

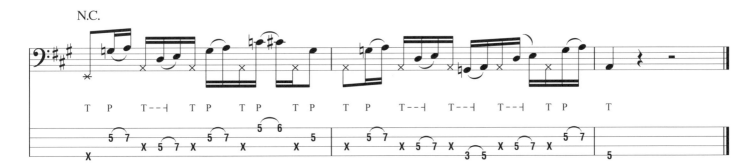

22. ABRAHAM LABORIEL, SR.

Born in Mexico City, Abraham Laboriel is one of the most recorded bass players in music history. With an estimated 4,000 recordings under his belt, the legendary session player has worked with artists ranging from Elton John and Dolly Parton to Lee Ritenour, Madonna, Michael Jackson, and Stevie Wonder. His recording credits as a bassist also include Pixar's *Ratatouille*, TV's *Breaking Bad*, and countless others. This piece, replete with arpeggiated lines, curlicues, and downright "slippery" passages, offers a glimpse into Abe's inimitable style.

Em7

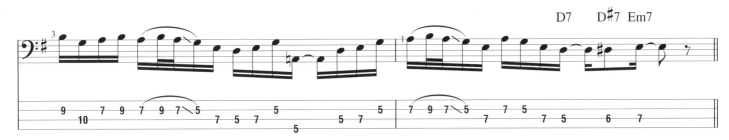

D7   D#7 Em7

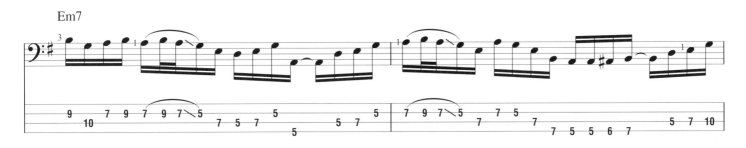

Em7

Em7

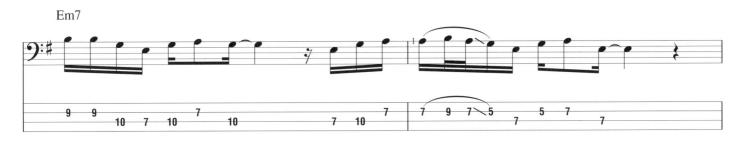

D7   D#7 E7

23. WILL LEE

Best known as the bassist for the David Letterman show—as well as for his Beatles tribute band, the Fab Faux—Will Lee has recorded with everyone from George Benson, James Brown, and the Brecker Brothers to Hiram Bullock, Chaka Khan, Sypro Gyra, Mike Stern, and too many others to count. This funky bass line with a bouncy feel makes use of heavy syncopation, heroic leaps, chordal fills, and 16th-note triplets.

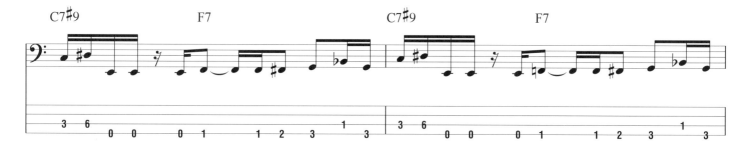

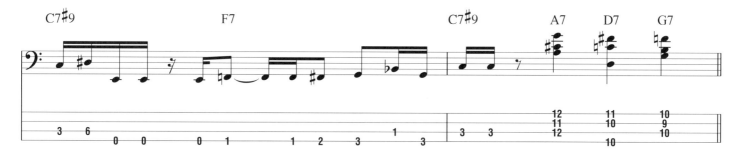

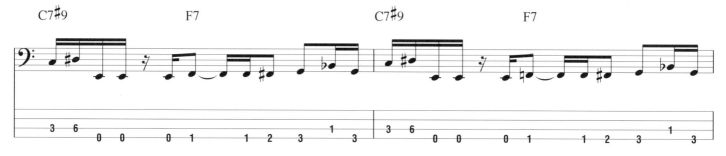

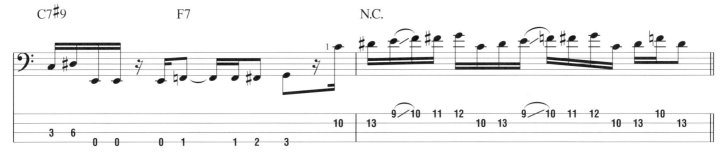

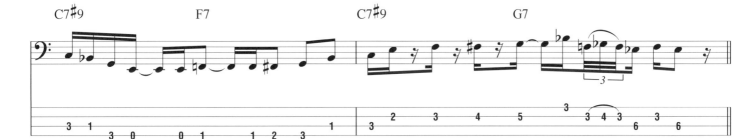

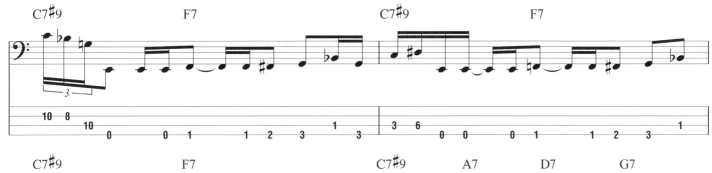

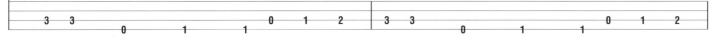

24. MESHELL NDEGEOCELLO

Pulling from a wide swath of musical influences, Meshell Ndegeocello's music incorporates elements of funk, jazz, hip-hop, and more. A truly unique and innovative player, Meshell's grooves, often understated, incorporate heavy use of electronics, grace notes, and surprising fingerboard jumps and chord changes.

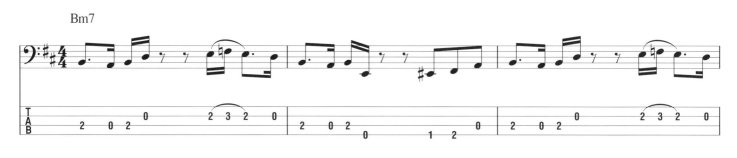

E7

Bm7

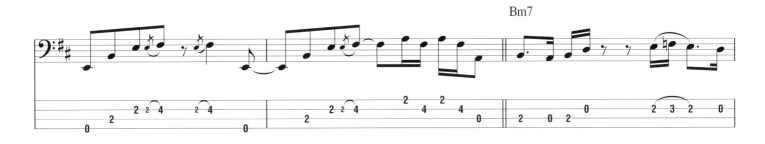

E7

Bm7

25. ROCCO PRESTIA

The force behind so many classic Tower of Power band grooves, Rocco's sound is characterized by his signature 16th-note, rapid-fire, "machine gun-style" bass lines. Whether he's playing repeated notes or chromatic runs, Rocco's playing invariably elevates the music's energy.

D7

D7

26. CHUCK RAINEY

One of the most prolific bass players of all time, Chuck Rainey has done thousands of recording sessions with many of the biggest names in the music world including Aretha Franklin, Quincy Jones, Steely Dan, and many others. Chuck's compelling grooves are enhanced by glissando lines, double stops, and his signature "half-step, tritone slide-up" (first popularized in his recording of TV's *The Jeffersons* theme).

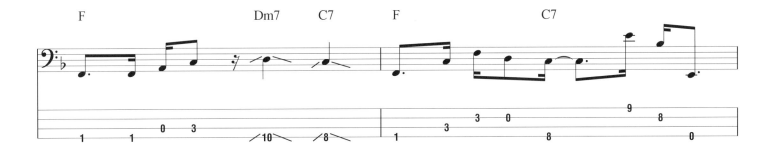

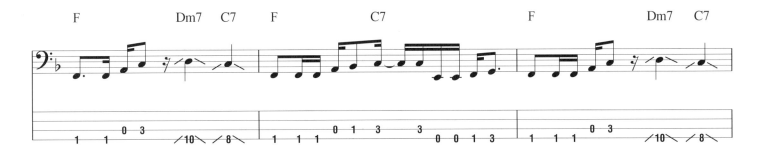

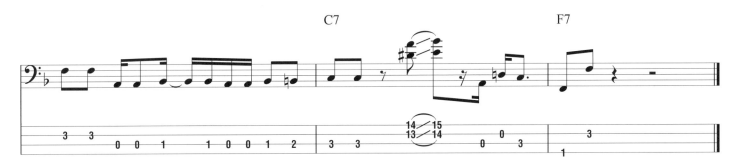

27. ESPERANZA SPALDING

A bona fide music superstar, Esperanza Spalding has captivated audiences across the globe with her original music, supplying electric and upright bass, and vocals, while picking up several Grammys along the way. Her bass lines can be busy, often containing unexpected leaps and jagged rhythms.

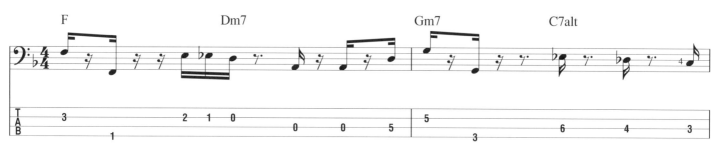

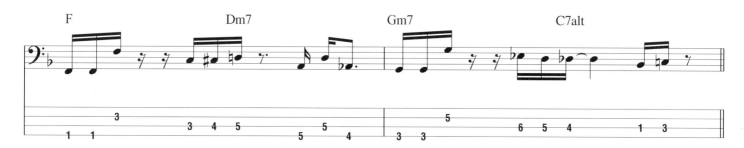

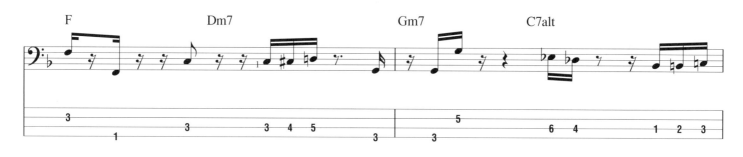

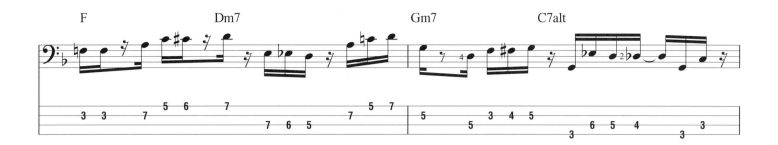

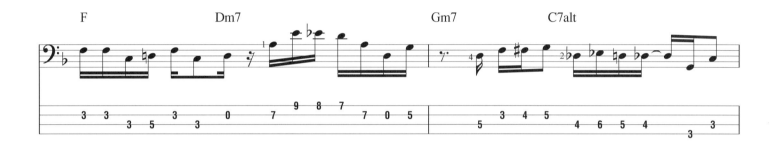

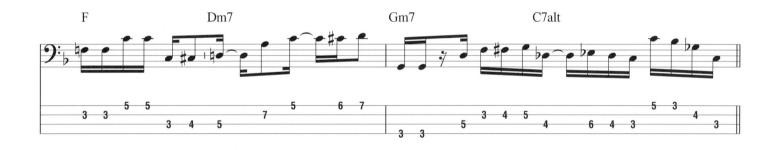

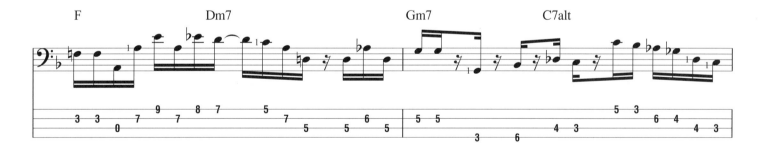

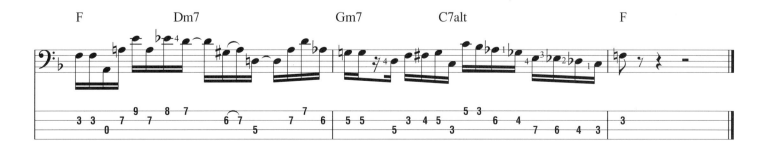

28. JAMAALADEEN TACUMA

An alumnus of the Ornette Coleman band and the avant-garde free jazz movement, Jamaaladeen Tacuma is also quite adept at "laying down the funk," making his music easily accessible to a wide audience. His grooves can be slow and dirty, interlaced with fast, busy fills.

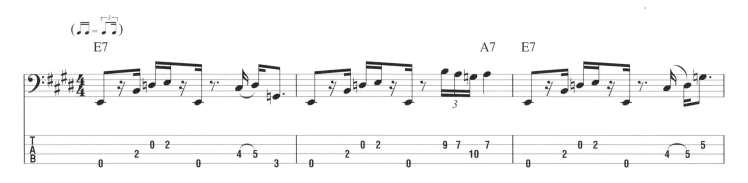

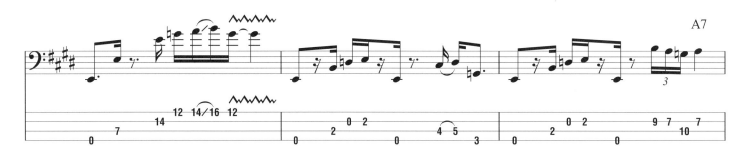

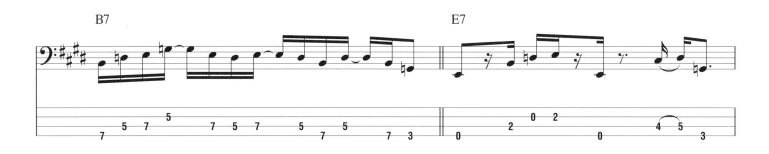

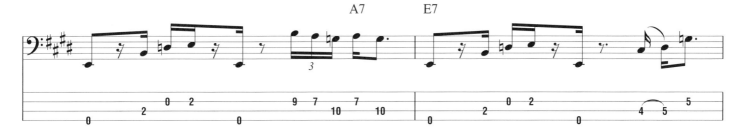

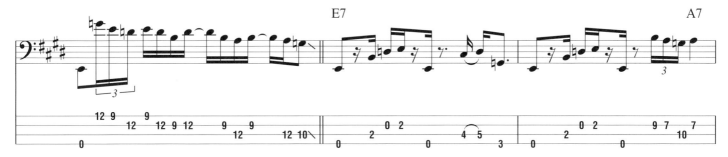

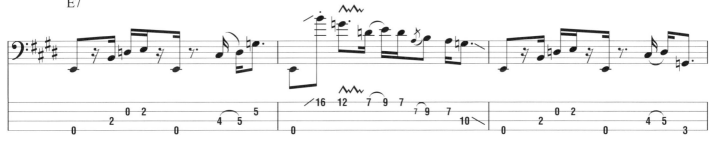

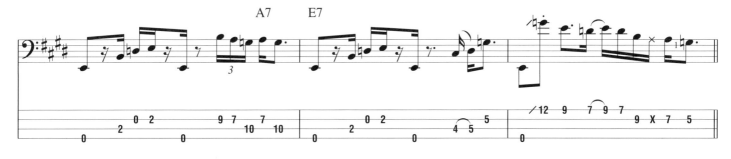

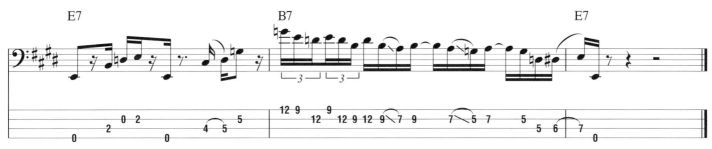

29. "READY" FREDDIE WASHINGTON

Throughout the course of a decades-long studio career, "Ready" Freddie Washington has done sessions with Anita Baker, Lionel Richie, Elton John, Whitney Houston, and many others. He also has a co-writing credit for Patrice Rushen's hit "Forget Me Nots" and has toured extensively with Steely Dan. Freddie's smooth grooves contain strong R&B elements with effective use of "dead" notes.

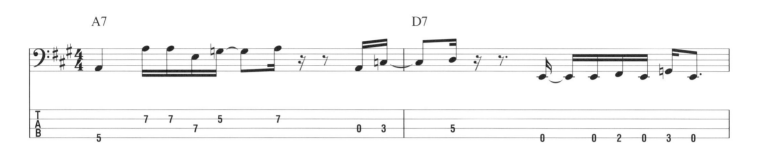

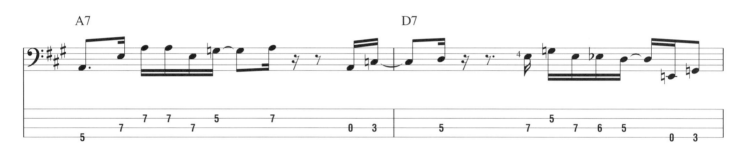

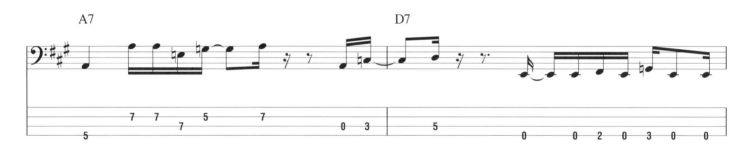

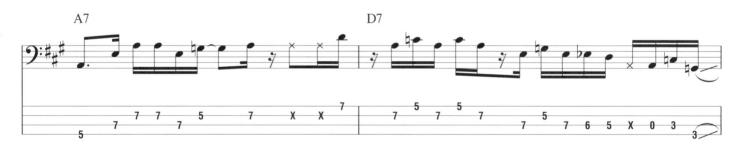

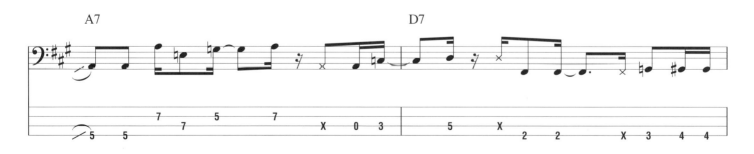

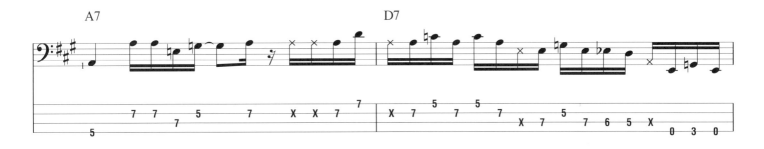

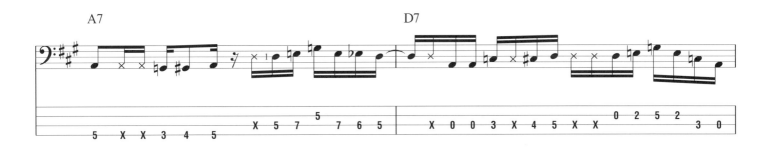

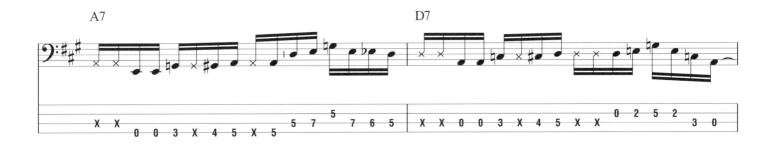

30. GARY WILLIS

Long held in high esteem for his prowess on the fretless bass, Gary Willis saw his profile rise in the '80s during his tenure with Scott Henderson and the Tribal Tech band. Willis has also worked with Wayne Shorter, Dennis Chambers, and Allan Holdsworth. His playing is characterized by a very light touch, bass ramp implementation, and distinctive muting techniques.

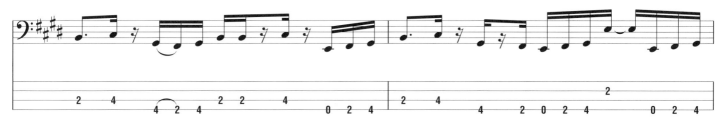

Straight

Hip-hop feel

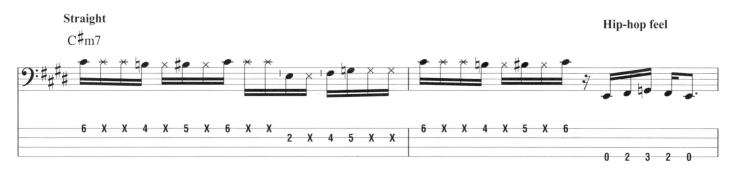

Straight

Hip-hop feel

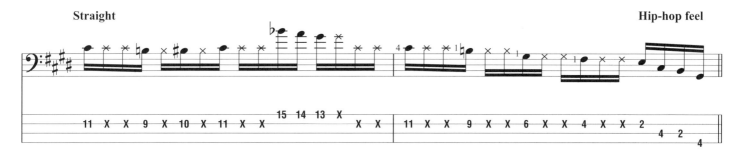

ABOUT THE AUTHOR

Photo by Randy Zdrojewski

Jon Liebman is a world-renowned bassist, composer, arranger, author, and educator. He has played electric and acoustic bass in every imaginable setting, from jazz gigs and club dates to full-scale concerts and internationally broadcast radio and TV shows. Jon has performed in many of the world's major concert venues, including New York's Madison Square Garden, L.A.'s Shrine Auditorium, and Tokyo's spectacular Suntory Hall (not to mention bull rings in Central America, amphitheaters in the Caribbean, and all kinds of off-beat settings across the globe).

Throughout the course of a career that began over thirty years ago, Jon has performed and/or toured with a wide range of musical acts including: Amy Grant, Cleo Laine, Buddy DeFranco, Billy Eckstine, Eartha Kitt, the Drifters, the Platters, the Coasters, the Chiffons, the Ink Spots, the Fifth Dimension, Julio Iglesias, José Feliciano, Ira Sullivan, Ralphe Armstrong, Gregory Hines, Theodore Bikel, and countless others. He has performed in the pit orchestras of many Broadway shows, including *Dreamgirls, Ain't Misbehavin', Phantom of the Opera, Les Misérables, Fiddler on the Roof, Oliver!, A Funny Thing Happened on the Way to the Forum, Golden Boy, Kiss of the Spider Woman, Annie*, and many others. He's also supplied bass tracks for major recording projects for clients including Ford, GM, and the NBA. In addition, Jon's big-band arrangements have been performed on *The Tonight Show, The Late Show*, and other programs.

As an educator, Jon's best-selling books and highly acclaimed online instruction courses have helped over 100,000 bassists improve their playing and are part of the curricula of many music schools, colleges, and universities throughout the world. *Funk/Jazz Bass* is Jon's tenth Hal Leonard book. His previous publications include *Funk Bass, Blues Bass, Bass Grooves: The Ultimate Collection, Bass Aerobics, Play Like Jaco Pastorius: The Ultimate Bass Lesson*, and *Bass Chops*.

Jon holds a Bachelor of Music degree in Jazz Studies & Contemporary Media from Wayne State University in Detroit, and a Master of Music degree in Studio Music & Jazz from the University of Miami in Coral Gables, Florida. Jon has spent time in California where he was active in the Los Angeles music scene as a performer and writer.

As the founder of Notehead MediaGroup, Jon conceived and developed the widely followed www.ForBassPlayersOnly.com website, one of the most popular sources in the world for online bass instruction. The site also features hundreds of one-on-one interviews Jon has conducted with some of the most famous bass players in the world. Jon lives in Michigan with his wife Mindy and has four children.